AF327568

# COUNT UNICO WILHELM VAN WASSENAER

ALBERT DUNNING

# COUNT UNICO WILHELM VAN WASSENAER

## (1692 - 1766)

A MASTER UNMASKED

or

THE PERGOLESI-RICCIOTTI PUZZLE SOLVED

TRANSLATED FROM DUTCH BY
JOAN RIMMER

# FOREWORD

In presenting this publication, I wish to express my indebtedness to a great number of friends and colleagues who bestowed their help on me, or who shared and encouraged my own enthusiasm for solving a problem which had already engaged my attention 18 years ago.

Among the former, Wouter van Leeuwen (*Amsterdam*) should be mentioned first: of all helpers, I owe him most. J.L. van der Klooster (*Den Haag*) most generously shared his profound knowledge of the history of the Van Wassenaer family with me. I must also thank Jhr.Dr.H.W.M.van der Wijck (*Doorn*) for his help. A number of improvements in my manuscript were suggested by the translator, Joan Rimmer (*Utrecht*).

Among the latter, I wish to thank particularly Jan and Marlou van Andel, Bernard van Beurden, Marius Flothuis, Frank Harrison, Frits Knuf, Jeanine Konings, Willem Noske, Anneke Uittenbosch and Maarten Vente.

*University of Utrecht 1980*                                                                 ALBERT DUNNING


## AUTHOR'S AND TRANSLATOR'S NOTE

The correct English form of the name and title of the subject of this book is *Unico Wilhelm Count of Wassenaer*. However, in view of the fact that this Netherlandish nobleman must now be internationally catalogued as a composer, it has been agreed that *Count Unico Wilhelm van Wassenaer* is a more practical form. Therefore, *Wassenaer, Count Unico Wilhelm van* is the appropriate catalogue and index entry.

# CONTENTS

# PART ONE
# INTRODUCTION

## 1. SIX CONCERTOS IN SEARCH OF AN AUTHOR

I t has been known for some time that the attribution to Giovanni Battista Pergolesi of six pieces generally called *Concertini* was dubious. These works, properly titled *Concerti armonici*, should have been described as anonymous.

Of itself, a label does not affect the quality of an object; it merely identifies it according to recognised conventions. This applies in historical musicology as much as in plant classification; names define characteristics and, at the same time, our understanding of them. Musical art-works, past and present, are classifiable from various viewpoints – *genre*, style, technique, period etc. The identitiy of the creator supplies one factor for the classificatory system and where this information is lacking – as with anonymous works[1] – our understanding is that much less. This has been the situation with the *Concerti armonici*, a peculiar situation, given the high artistic quality of the pieces, which is acknowledged both by musicologists and by an international music-loving public. This public which is often thought to be uncritical has, in the long term, continued to appreciate these works, both when they were and when they were not attached to a 'great name'. As is well known in the music business, doubtful authorship generally hinders just appreciation of a work, or may even alter that appreciation according to the degree of acceptance that it was or was not the work of a 'great' composer. The fate of pieces 'attributed to' or 'copies of works by' Bach, Mozart, Haydn and Beethoven – for example, the oblivion to which the so-called Jena symphony is now consigned – confirms this. As if roses by any other name are less fragrant! The *Concerti armonici*, however, have become a staple part of 20th–century repertory, with countless concert performances and recordings over the past 40 years.

Both 'external' philological criteria and 'internal' stylistic criteria are involved in decisions about the authenticity of musical works. Stylistic research, with its subjectively-chosen criteria, can at most answer the question of who an author could be. Actual identity, to the exclusion of all other candidates, can ultimately only be attested by external criteria – those of unassailable sources. Where these are lacking, musicologists have no tools of stylistic analysis which can be equally determinative.[2]

Problems of attribution and authenticity form an important part of the older discipline of art history. Creators of unsigned works are identified with finely-graded distinctions like 'pupil of', 'from the studio of', 'from the school of', etc. In this field, unlike musicology which has virtually no concept of a 'connoisseur', great careers have been made and broken; for example, in the course of the Van Meegeren affair. During the last few decades, however, there has been an increasing tendency among art historians to restrict the importance of intuitive elements as compared with philological criteria.[3]

The world fame of the *Concerti armonici* is without doubt due in the first place to their high musical quality. Next – and this factor must not be underestimated – the attribution to Pergolesi has not been detrimental, though it can equally be said that it did not damage his reputation, either. The real creator of these works, however, did not merely avoid publicity; he took active steps to remain anonymous. The high calibre of these pieces plus the anonymity of the author has raised problems to which various solutions have been proposed at various times. Here, in chronological order, are the earlier attemps to solve the puzzle of authorship.

In 1740, an edition of the *Concerti armonici* appeared in Den Haag[4] with the following title (see *plate* 1): *'VI. CONCERTI/ARMONICI/A/QUATTRO VIOLINI OBLIGATI, ALTO VIOLA/ VIOLONCELLO OBLIGATO E BASSO CONTINUO/DEDICATI/ALL'ILLUSTRISSIMO*

1. Title page of the *Concerti armonici*, published by Carlo Ricciotti, Den Haag 1740.

SIGNORE/IL SIGNORE CONTE/DI BENTINCK/ &c. &c. &c./DAL SUO HUMILISSIMO SERVITORE, C. RICCIOTTI,/DETTO BACCICCIA, E STAMPATI A SUE SPESE,/ALLA HAYE, IN HOLLANDA'. Note that Carlo Ricciotti appears here as publisher and dedicator, and no composer's name is given. According to the custom of that time, the next page carries a note to the dedicatee, in this case Willem, graaf Bentinck (see *plate 2*):

'Illustrissimo Signore
Le lettere dedicatorie non agiongano alcun merito alle virtù, ne tampoco alle dignità delle persone, à cui son' dirette, e sarà più eloquente il nome di V.S. Illustrissima nel frontispicio di questa mia, che tutti gl'elogj, e frasi più sublimi d'un sapiente Autore. Mi restringo sol donque à suplicarla d'accettar tanto più volontieri questo lavoro che è parto d'un Illustre mano, che V.S. Illustrissima stima, ed honora, ed à cui ne son debitore per suo reguardo. Degnisi finalmente ricever colla sua solita bontà

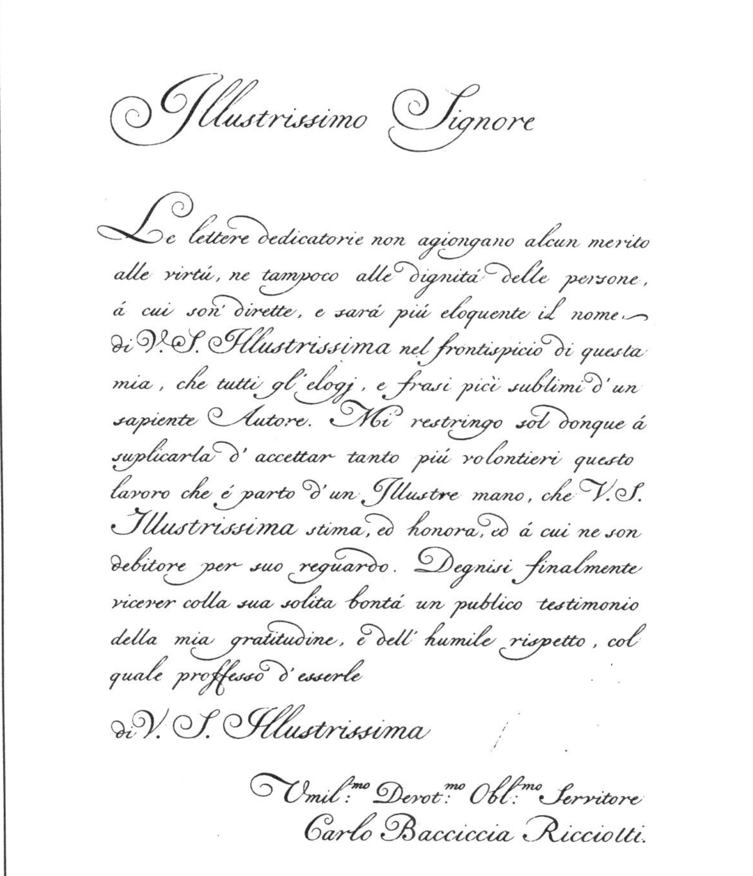

2. Dedication from Carlo Ricciotti to Count Willem Bentinck.

un publico testimonio della mia gratitudine, e dell' humile rispetto, col quale proffesso d'esserle di
V.S. Illustrissima
Umil:^mo Devot:^mo Obl:^mo Servitore
    Carlo Bacciccia Ricciotti.'

Bentinck is here asked to accept these works which have come from an 'Illustrious hand' already honoured and esteemed by him. The word *Illustre* is certainly used here in its 18th-century sense of 'honourable' and 'of high social rank', not in the later sense of 'famous'. The composer was described as 'a distinguished Gentleman' in a concert advertisement in the *Haagsche Courant* on August 18, 1749, which announced a performance of some *Concerti armonici*: 'M^r Sieber, Manager of the New Vaux-Hall, announces that his Concerts will take place as usual on Tuesday, Thursday and Saturday and that Mr. Groneman, Director of Music in the New Vaux-Hall, at the request of several

3. Title page of the *Concerti armonici*, published by Walsh, London 1755.

Gentleman and Amateurs, will have performed sundry fine Concertos, among them certain *Concerti armonici* composed by a distinguished Gentleman and printed by C.Ricciotti, detto Batticcia.'[5]

Carlo Ricciotti detto Bacciccia played a leading part in the mysterious production, since he was the intermediary between the composer and the recipient of the works, Bentinck. As far back as 1702 Ricciotti can be found under the name Charles Bachiche in a French opera company in Den Haag;[6] he belonged to it until 1725, ultimately being its director. It is not known what functions he fulfilled between that date and the time of his death in Den Haag in 1756, though family records suggest that he remained in that city. No trace has been found of his activity as a composer.

At a time when literary and musical creations were not protected by law, publishers could freely pirate each others publications; a so-called licence to print only gave a publisher protection against piracy where the jurisdiction of the licence-giver held good. Thus, in 1755, the London publisher Walsh was able to reprint the *Concert armonici*.[7] In this edition, Ricciotti was elevated to the position of composer (see *plate 3*).

It is not so long ago that Ricciotti was still seriously advocated as the composer of the *Concerti armonici*[8], despite the doubly absurd implication that he would have been presenting himself to Bentinck as *Illustre* and also been indebted to himself.[9]

Ricciotti's edition had raised problems in several respects: also cataloguing was difficult. Among thousands of musical items offered for sale at an auction in Den Haag in 1759 were *'VI Concerti Armonici, a quattro Violini Obligati, Alto Viola, Violoncello Obligato è Basse Continuo'*, attributed to Willem de Fesch.[10] Was this due to carelessness in compiling the catalogue or to an assumption on the part of the auctioneer? Willem de Fesch was certainly one of the worthier Netherlandish composers of that time; but to anyone even slightly acquainted with his work, his authorship of the *Concerti armonici* is ruled out on grounds of style and quality.

The search for the real author is a tale in itself. In England, the *Concerti armonici* were still popular to some extent long after Ricciotto's publication in 1740[11], and in 1822, William Crotch, Heather Professor of Music in the University of Oxford, stated that the name Ricciotti was 'said to have been assumed by an Italian nobleman'.[12]

In the 19th century, renewed interest in the music of earlier times prompted countless publications of 'old music'. Also, thousands of scores were prepared from old part books. Many of these manuscript scores can still be found in libraries all over the world. Those who are acquainted with them can only be impressed by the energy and industry of 19th-century historical music enthusiasts. Today, however, it can be seen that, despite their enthusiasm, their methods were often defective or inappropriate. It is in this light that a manuscript score attributed to Handel or Pergolesi (now in the Library of Congress) must be seen.[13] This copy, which bears neither date nor copyist's name and whose paper lacks a watermark, must have been made in the first half of the 19th century. It has two title pages, on identical paper and written in identical ink in the same hand. The first and older title page has Handel's name: '6/Concertini[14]/Septetti/Per 4 Violino, Alto. Violoncello/e Basso continuo/in partitura/del F.G. Handel/NB Pergolesi.'[15] This was discovered only in 1952 when the second title page, which had been stuck over the first, was lifted. The second and later title page reads: '6/Concertini/Per 4 Violini. Alto. Violoncello/e/Basso continuo/ in partizione/del Pergolesi'. This page carries the stamp 'F.Commer' and an *ex libris 'De la Collection de/Musique de Monsieur François Lessel'*. This François Lessel (*c* 1780-1835)[16] was a Polish composer who had at one time been influenced by Joseph Haydn in Vienna. Probably Lessel prepared the score, which later came into the possession of Franz Commer (1813–1887)[17], a man of considerable reputation as a collector and editor of old music, chiefly from the 16th century. The Library of Congress acquired this manuscript in 1908, probably in an auction at Leo Liepmanssohn, the Berlin auctioneers. The defective Italian in this copy shows that it was not of Italian origin.

The library of the Paris Conservatoire possesses a manuscript of these *Concertini* which must have been written at the end of the 19th century or the beginning of the 20th century. From the order of items, identical mistakes etc., it appears to be a copy of the Washington manuscript.[18] The same is true of a manuscript that once belonged to the late Hans Hoesch of Hagen, Westphalia, who had acquired it shortly after the first world war from the estate of the musicologist Erich Prieger (1849-1913).[19]

The attributions to Handel and Pergolesi in these manuscripts are of little significance; probably all we are dealing with here is the conjecture of the copyist of the oldest manuscript, now in Washington. Despite the shakiness of the attribution to Pergolesi, the *Concerti armonici*, now named

*Concertini*, were published with Pergolesi's name firmly attached, notably in the Collected Edition of his works, and given new life in countless concert performances and recordings.[20]

Musicology is now a firmly established discipline, and musicologists are rather more critical in assessing the reliability of sources than were the enthusiasts of the 19th century. Is is, therefore, not surprising that doubts have been raised about the attribution of these *Concertini* to Pergolesi, the more so since it is now clear that they are, in fact, the *Concerti armonici* originally published by Ricciotti with the mysterious indication that they were the work of an 'Illustrious hand'.[21] From the moment it became known that, on philological, let alone stylistic grounds the *Concerti armonici* could hardly have been the work of Pergolesi, the subject was wide open to speculation and hypothesis.

The highly reputable musicologist Hans Joachim Moser proposed Johann Adam Birkenstock as the composer[22], who, according to Johann Gottfried Walthers *Musikalisches Lexikon oder musikalische Bibliothek* (Leipzig 1732, p. 95) in 1730 'Sonate à Violino solo e Continuo; ingleichen XII Concerti à 4 Violini obligati, Alto Viola, Violoncello e Basso Continuo, nach Amsterdam geschicket, welche in etlichen Monaten ans Licht treten werden'. The Amsterdam publisher may well have been Le Cène, though according to that firm's catalogues, these 12 Concertos with intrumentation similar to that of the *Concerti armonici* never appeared.[23] This hypothesis rests solely on similarity of instrumentation, and that is hardly a weighty argument. Here, too, stylistic differences between the *Concerti armonici* and Birkenstock's work are so great that Moser's hypothesis can be termed no more than a good try. Above all, Birkenstock does not fit the composer's social rank as defined in Ricciotti's dedicatory letter; he could in no way have been described as 'Illustre'.

In 1963, I formulated a hypothesis that must now be discarded. The few clues to the composer's true identity – that he was of high rank and, since he was esteemed and honoured by Bentinck, must have been known to him personally – suggested that the answer to the puzzle might lie in Bentinck's personal papers, a great quantity of which have been preserved.[24] Eventually, I proposed Fortunato Chelleri as a serious candidate. Bentinck knew him well, and as *Hofrat** to the King of Sweden, a position which entitled him to be addressed as 'Excellency', he also fulfilled in some sense the 'Illustre' requirement. Stylistically, one could say no more than that the attribution was not impossible. This hypothesis is now demonstrably mistaken.

---

* Court counsellor

# PART ONE
# INTRODUCTION

## 2. THE AUTHOR IDENTIFIED

I n the Castle of Twickel (see *plates 5 and 6*) in Delden in the province of Overijssel, there is a manuscript score of the *Concerti armonici* which dates from the first half of the 18th century.[25] This manuscript has a foreword which solves all problems (see *plate 4*): 'Partition de mes concerts, gravez par le Sr. Ricciotti, surnommé Bachiche. Ces concerts ont été composez en differens tems entre les anées 1725 et 1740. A mesure qu'ils furent faits, je les portai au concert etabli a la Haye, entre Mess[rs] Bentincq, moy, et quelques Seigneurs etrangers. Le dit Bachiche y jouait le 1[r] violon. Je luy permis d'en prendre successivement copie. La demie douzaine etant complette, il me demanda permission de les faire graver. Sur mon refus reiteré, il implora le secours de M[r] Bentincq de Roon, sur les fortes instances duquel, je me rendis enfin, a condition que mon nom n'y paratrait point, et qu'il pourait y mettre le sien, ce qu'il fit. Il voulut me le dedier, je le refusai absolument, sur quoy M[r] Bentincq lui dit de les luy dedier. C'est ainsi que ces concerts sont devenus publies, contre mon intention. Il y a du passable, du mediocre, du mauvais. Sans la publication, j'en aurais, peut être, corrigé les défauts, mais d'autres occupations ne m'ont pas laissé le loisir de m'y amuser, et j'aurais fait tort a l'Editeur.'

These lines are written in the hand of Unico Wilhelm, *Graaf van Wassenaer, Heer*[a] *van Twickel* etc., and the manuscript is in what was formerly his private library.[26] This Netherlandish composer of six master works is completely unknown to music historians. Who was he?

Unico Wilhelm, count of Wassenaer, was born into one of the oldest noble families of the Province of Holland.[27] A branch of the Van Raephorst line, it descended from Philip van Wassenaer, (Philips de Wasnare) and had been known since 1200. One notable member of the family was Jacob, Baron van Wassenaer, who earned great fame in the days of Netherlandish maritime power. Unico Wilhelm was born in the Castle of Twickel on November 2, 1692, and was baptised in the church in Delden. His parents were Jacob van Wassenaer (1645-1715) – whose full titles were *Jacob des Heiligen Roomse Rijksgraaf van Wassenaer*[b], *Baanderheer*[c], *van Wassenaer, Heer van Obdam, Hensbroek, Spierdijk, Wogmeer, Zuidwijk, Kernhem en Schonauwen* – and Adriana Sophie van Raesfelt, Vrouwe[d] *van Lage en Twickel* ( † 1694).[28] To this pair, married in 1676, seven children were born, five of whom reached adulthood. The eldest was Agnes Anna Theodora (1678-1746); after her came Amadea Isabella (1681-1750) who never married and Johan Hendrik (1683-1745) also unmarried, who will appear later in this study. The two youngest children were Isabelle Aemilia Charlotte (1689-1740), who married Guido Pape, Marquis de St. Auban in 1723, and our Unico Wilhelm. By birth or inheritance he acquired the following titles at various times in his life: *H.R. Rijksgraaf van Wassenaer, Baanderheer van Wassenaer, Vrijheer*[e] *van Lage, Heer van Twickel, Obdam, Hensbroek, Spierdijk, Wogmeer, Zuidwijk, Kernhem, Weldam en Olidam.*

Unico Wilhelm no doubt passed his early years in the parental house in Den Haag and the Castle of Twickel. Though his elder brother Johan Hendrik accompanied his father to Berlin during his

---

[a]  Fr. *seigneur.* There is no modern English equivalent, though the old 'lord of the manor' and still-current Scotch 'laird' convey a comparable meaning of landed proprietor or estate owner.

[b]  Count of the Holy Roman Empire.

[c]  Banneret: a nobleman entitled to lead men into battle under his own banner.

[d]  The female equivalent of *Heer.*

[e]  Roughly comparable with Baron.

4. Foreword by Unico Wilhelm van Wassenaer in the manuscript of the *Concerti armonici*.

term as ambassador there (May 1699 - April 1702), it is not known whether Unico Wilhelm did also. [29] But he and his sisters did accompany their father during his first term in Düsseldorf (October 1707 - April 1709) at the court of the Elector Johann Wilhelm von der Pfalz, with whom Jacob van Wassenaer had a friendly relationship. [30] The names of Agostino Steffani, Arcangelo Corelli, Attilio Ariosti, Antonio Draghi, Giuseppe Antonio Bernabei, Francesco Antonio Mamiliano Pistocchi, George Frederick Handel and many others well known to music historians were connected with that magnificent Maecenas. [31] The musical atmosphere of the court in Düsseldorf, which ranked as one of the most splendid in Europe, must have had considerable influence on the almost 15-year-old son of the ambassador of the Dutch Republic.

5. The Castle of Twickel in 1727.

Agostino Steffani, who held various musical and political positions in the Düsseldorf court while the Van Wassenaers were there, was a trusted friend of the Elector. A characteristic European musical personality of the time, he must have been a significant figure during the short, but perhaps formative period of the young Netherlandish nobleman's life which was spent in Düsseldorf. At that time, Unico's native land had nothing as musically lavish as the court of the Elector Palatine.

In April 1709, the family returned to Den Haag and lived in the old family house at the corner of the Kneuterdijk. [32] On April 14, 1710, Unico Wilhelm made the formal adult profession of Christian faith in the Walloon (*i.e.* French speaking) church. [33] On September 18 of the same year, he was inscribed as a student in Leiden University. [34] It is known from the letters of his tutor, Carrier, that he did in fact study there, at least in 1712-13 [35] and followed courses in law, among other subjects, under Professor Ph.R.Vitrarius. In 1713, he and his elder brother Johan Hendrik paid a short visit to Düsseldorf, where his father was again in residence. [36] In 1714 he legally came of age in Holland and

6. The Castle of Twickel in 1729.

Overijssel, the provinces where the family had property. On April 13 and 14 of the same year, the Castle of Twickel was visited by the Elector of Hanover, who was to be crowned king of England in the following October. As King George I, he paid another visit in 1727.[38]

At his father's death, Unico Wilhelm inherited the Twickel estates, and took formal possession of them on October 13, 1717.[39] By the same inheritance, he became entitled to enter the *ridderschap** of Overijssel and was formally invested in April 1717.[40] Shortly after this the young nobleman must have commenced his Grand Tour as he was not available for state meetings in the Netherlands in 1717 and 1718.[41] A letter written in 1732, recommending two cousins to Cardinal Corsini in Rome,

*  Literally: knighthood; an administrative assembly of nobles.

7. Count Willem Bentinck (miniature in a brooch).

gives an idea of part of his itinerary. Unico Wilhelm referred to 'les relations que j'ai eu l'honneur d'avoir avec V.Em. en Hollande, en Allemagne mais surtout à Paris dans les années 1717 et 1718'.[42] Towards the end of 1718, he was back in the Netherlands; the Duchess of Portland wrote to Unico's brother, Johan Hendrik in December 'Je vous félicite du retour de monsieur le Comte de Twickle. Je suis fachée qu'il n'a pas voulu passer quelque peu de ce temps qu'il a été éloigné de vous ici car... (*unreadable*) faite une très grande plaisir de le voir en Engleterre'.[43] Apart from Paris, it is not certain which lands and cities were visited, though the above letter indicates that England was not among them. No doubt he followed the customary routes; Italy certainly – perhaps Venice, Florence and Rome – and probably Vienna or Prague. Whatever the itinerary was in detail, a great number of musical impressions must have been left with the young man, some of which are relevant to the artistic background of the *Concerti armonici.*

The importance of the Grand Tour to a musically impressionable youth is apparent from the

8. Count Willem Bentinck (crayon drawing after Liotard).

experience of someone who was soon to come into the life of 'M$^r$ de Twickle' (as he was generally called) and whose name is closely connected with the *Concerti armonici*, namely Willem Bentinck (see *plates 7 and 8*). Willem Bentinck, *Heer van Rhoon and Pendrecht*, was born at Schoonheeten on October 17, 1704, to the Duke of Portland (1649-1709) and his second wife, Jane Martha Temple. [44] Brought up at first in England, he and his younger brother Charles came to the Netherlands in June 1717, to the estates left to them by their father. Unico Wilhelm's elder brother, Johan Hendrik, graaf van Wassenaer-Obdam, was Willem Bentinck's guardian, and Carrier (who had earlier taught Unico Wilhelm) and later, Bernège, were his tutors. [45] Extensive correspondence between guardian, tutors and pupil on one hand, and Bentinck's mother, the Duchess of Portland on the other [46], tells us a good deal about early contacts between the young Bentinck and the Van Wassenaer family, particularly M$^r$ de Twickle, who was his senior by 12 years. The two young nobleman shared a love of music and indeed music played a considerable part in aristocratic life at that time. Where Bentinck

16

was concerned, we know that he took singing and harpsichord lessons, and also violin lessons, the addition of which greatly displeased his guardian.[47] Quirinus van Blankenburg must have been his harpsichord teacher[48] and his violin teacher was none other than Bachiche, *i.e.* Ricciotti. 'My chief diversions are musick and walking' wrote the young Bentinck to his mother.[49]

Bentinck had rich musical experiences in the course of his own Grand Tour in the years 1726-1728.[50] His brother Charles was also a music-lover and, like Willem, a member of the music-making circle in Den Haag; Egidio Romualdo Duni dedicated his Trio sonatas, Opus I to him (*c* 1745).[51] The second edition of the *Clavecimbel- en Orgelboek* of Quirinus van Blankenburg[52] was dedicated to Willem by the publisher, Berkoske (who described him as a virtuoso), as were the Symphonies, Opus II of the court composer Francesco Pasquale Ricci.[53] Bentinck retained this love of music throughout his life, and in old age, along with his son Anton, he met the Mozart family during their stay in the Netherlands.[54] During his early years in Den Haag, Willem Bentinck was on the most intimate terms with the Van Wassenaers. Johan Hendrik, his sisters Amadea and Charlotte, the latter now married to the Marquis of St. Auban, and M[r] de Twickle 'ce sont là les uniques maisons qu'il fréquente', so Bernège informed Willem's mother.[55] Regularly on Mondays, the two young men entertained a select gathering for a musical evening, alternately M[r] de Twickel at his town house and Willem Bentinck at Sorghvliet or at his town house in the Lange Voorhout. 'Le concert de musique se tint Lundy dernier chez Vous... je vais avoir l'honneur de vous nommer, Madame, tous ceux qui y etoient, et qui se doivent trouver chez M[r] de Twickle Lundy prochain. Les dames etoient Mad[e] de Twickle et Mad[elle] Goslinga sa sœur, Mad[e] de Reck, et Mad[elle] de Wassenaer. Parmi les Messieurs se trouvèrent Messieurs Finck, de Twickle, Chancour, Osorio, Messieurs de Saumaise & M[r] de St. Auban. On eut beaucoup de musique, beaucoup de Thé et de Caffé'.[56] These were doubtless the company at the 'concert etabli entre les Messieurs Bentincq, moy et quelques Seigneurs étrangers', mentioned in the note at the beginning of the manuscript in the Castle of Twickel. The relationship between Willem Bentinck and the various members of the Van Wassenaer family must have been warm, even though Johan Hendrik van Wassenaer's guardianship of the somewhat boisterous young man raised certain problems.[57] Bentinck countered the accusation that he had inappropriately close contacts with the opera company in Den Haag (almost certainly Ricciotti's company)[58] with the justification that he never went there alone, but always in the company of other people such as M[r] de Twickle.[59] Bentinck's visit to Unico Wilhelm at the Castle of Twickel in 1729[60] was surely neither the first nor the only visit there. In later years, political differences separated these two men whose common love of music had brought them into such intimate contact in the 1720s;[61] opposite views chilled their relationship.[62]

The 1720s must have been a relatively care-free period for the two young noblemen; as yet, neither carried any public responsibility. The first hint of Unico Wilhelm's activity as a composer dates from 1725 and comes from a trustworthy source – the pen of his elder brother.[63] In his *Etrennes* (New Year greeting to his family and friends) he teased the Walloon clergyman Saurin and Willem Bentinck among others, and also requested M[r] de Twickle 'de ne pas contrefaire si naturellement l'hebeté comme cela lui arrive par fois, item de ne pas epuiser toutes les facultés de son ame sur du papier reglé, item de troquer ses notes contre des mots, ...'. These lines show how great the now 32-year-old Unico's obsession with 'music paper' must have been, and the date of this exhortation coincides with the beginning of the composition of the *Concerti armonici*.

A sketch of the rest of Unico Wilhelm's life is necessary before further investigation of his

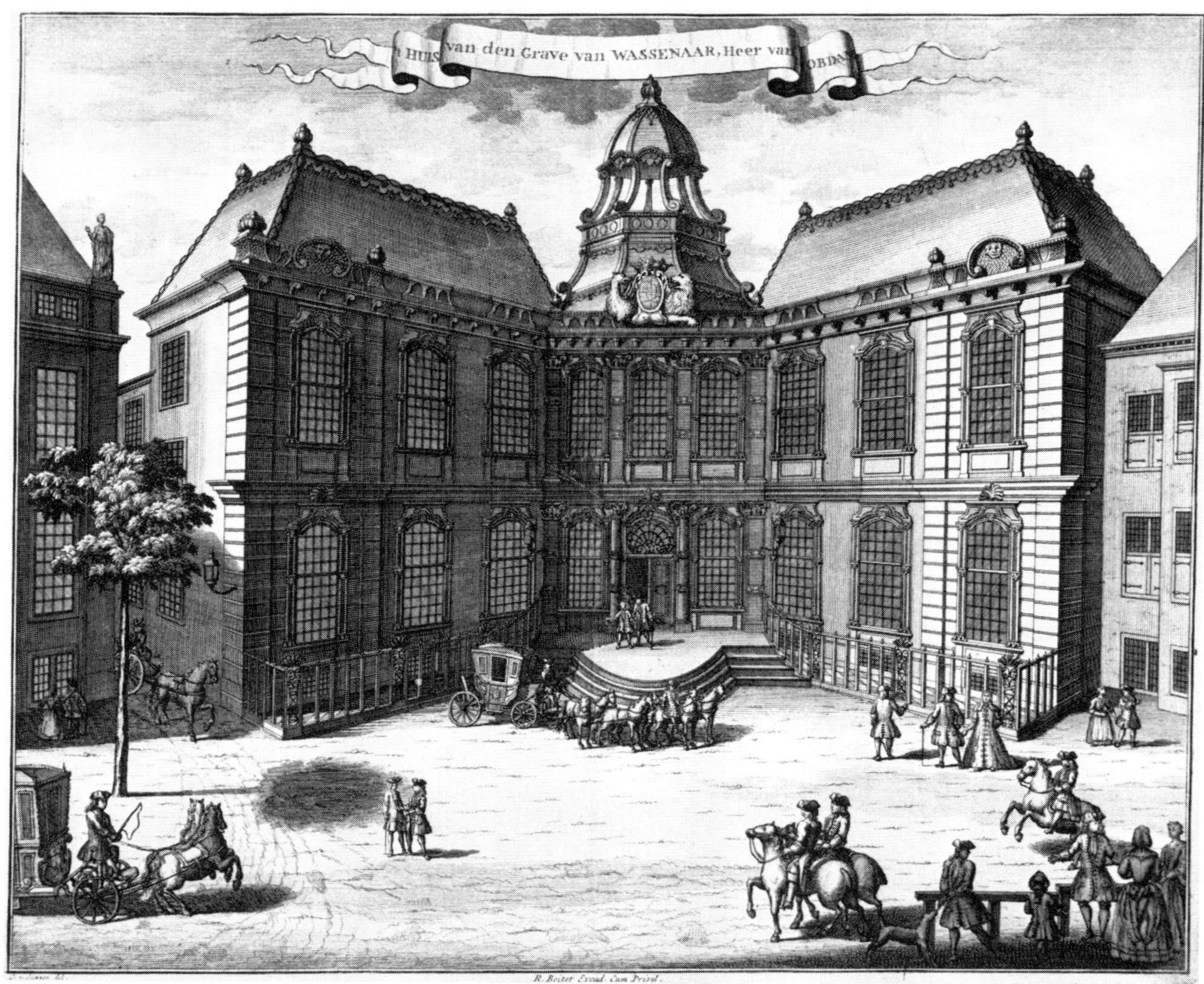


9. The house on the corner of the Kneuterdijk, in which Count Unico Wilhelm van Wassenaer lived from 1746 onwards.

composing activities. He married an aristocratic Frisian girl, Dodonea Lucia van Goslinga, daughter of Sicco van Goslinga and Johanetta Isabella, baroness of Schwartzenberg and Hohenlandsberg, on September 26, 1723, at Dongjum in Friesland. Three sons were born of this marriage, Jan Jacob (1724-1779), Sicco (1731-1750) and Carel George (1733-1800).[64] In 1723, Unico Wilhelm was appointed *Hoogheemraad** of Rijnland. In 1724 he became a member of the Board of the Admiralty and in 1734 a director of the East India Company.[65] These positions entailed virtually permanent residence in Den Haag and in the mid-1720s, the young married pair must have settled there, probably in a property on the east side of Noordeinde which no longer exists.[66] They were certainly

*  High office in the Commission of Dike Control.

10. Count Unico Wilhelm van Wassenaer (oil painting by Jan Palthe).

there in 1742, when Unico's annual income was estimated as 16,000 guilders and the rentable value of the house at 975 guilders. The establishment then had 4 horses and 11 servants.[67] After the death of the unmarried Johan Hendrik in 1745, Unico Wilhelm moved into the big house on the Kneuterdijk, designed by the architect Daniel Marot (see *plate 9*), and remained there till his death.[68] After his admission to the *ridderschap* of Holland on February 7, 1746, Unico Wilhelm was appointed to high office at the international level. He was ambassador in Paris in 1744 and in Cologne in 1746, in which year he also represented the Republic of the United Provinces of the Netherlands at the Congress of Breda.[69] (His republican allegiance was in opposition to that of his old friend Bentinck, who supported extension of the hereditary functions of the Prince of Orange.)[70] In the *Duitse Orde**

* A German religious-chivalrous order founded in 1190.

19

11. Count Unico Wilhelm van Wassenaer (oil painting by J.F. Douven, 1719).

he was successively *jonkheer* (1732), *commandeur* (1733), *coadjutor* (1753) and *landcommandeur* (1762), and his portrait in the garb of that order, painted by Jan Palthe, can still be seen (*plate 10*).[71] Besides this portrait, which is the property of that division of the order to which Unico Wilhelm belonged, there are two paintings which belong now to the Twickel Foundation (see *plates 11 and 12*). Unico Wilhelm must have sat for the painter J.F. Douven in Düsseldorf in 1719;[72] the portrait painted by George de Marees in 1745 was the model for an engraving by J. Houbraken.[73]

Unico Wilhelm died on November 9, 1766 and was buried on the 13th in the St. Jacobskerk in Den Haag. His wife died in Den Haag in January, 1769.

Unico Wilhelm, graaf van Wassenaer: Sunday musician or near-professional? Either way, as creator of the *Concerti armonici*, he is an interesting figure, and knowledge of his identity and background can bring a new dimension to study of these works.

12. Count Unico Wilhelm van Wassenaer (oil painting by George de Marees, 1745).

Documentary evidence about his musical horizons is not abundant. The influences of the court at Düsseldorf, of his Grand Tour and of the aristocratic, cosmopolitan sphere into which he was born and in which he worked as a diplomat[74], can only be surmised, though they must have been significant. More concrete are his family background (for example, an earlier member, Jacob van Duivenvoorde-Obdam was the dedicatee of Cornelis Schuyt's *Hymeneo overo madrigali* of 1611[75]) and his known contacts as a young man with professional musicans of the calibre of Ricciotti and Quirinus van Blankenburg. It can be imagined that Unico Wilhelm, as well as Willem Bentinck, took harpsichord lessons, and perhaps composition lessons also, from Quirinus van Blankenburg. The library from the Castle of Twickel, which now contains relatively little music, still has some which has survived from an originally much greater collection. After the death of Unico Wilhelm's unmarried son, Jacob Jan, on December 25, 1779, many of his books were sold. The auction catalogue[76] contained two pages of musical works (see *plate 13*) of which a good number must

21

13. From the Catalogue of an auction of books which had belonged to Count Jacob Jan van Wassenaer, 1788.



formerly have belonged to Unico Wilhelm. As evidenced there, the musical orientation was strongly towards France.[77] Among dramatic works, those of French origin (Lully, Stuck) greatly outnumbered those of Handel and Bononcini. In instrumental music, there was a preponderance of solo sonatas (Guerini, Tessarini, Mossi, Avantano and Mascitti) and trio sonatas (Corelli and Valentini). One unusual item (No. 19) was a 'Cantate Françoise, composée par M. le Comte de la Lippe Schaumborg, à la Haye, Avril 1727', a work by the lover of Willem Bentinck's wife.[78]

The music which remains in the library appears to be a residue after numerous bequests, sales and removals. (The manuscript score of the *Concerti armonici*, reproduced on pp. 35 and one other manuscript are exceptional;[79] it may well be that successive heirs, still aware of Unico Wilhelm's activities as a composer, did not wish to sell these scores). For example, there is a copy of the voice parts of the cantata *Heraclite et Democrite* by Jean Baptiste Stuck (published by Ballard in Paris in 1711 as *Cantates françaises*) in Unico Wilhelm's own hand, with his own signature (see *plate 14*), and works

22

14. Copy of the bass part of the cantate 'Heraclite et Democrite' by Jean Baptiste Stuck, in the hand of Count Unico Wilhelm van Wassenaer.

by Destouches (*Amadis de Grèce*), Campra (*Hesione*) and Bernier (*Cantates françaises*, also with Unico Wilhelm's signature) which confirm the French orientation seen in the sale catalogue. Francesco Guerini's violin sonatas Opus I en II[80], Telemann's six sonatas for violin and harpsichord (1718) and six trios (published by Kenckel), Tartini's violin sonatas Opus II (Roman edition), Geminiani's sonatas Opus I[81] and Senaillé's violin sonatas Opus I[82] (both published by Roger in Amsterdam), and Locatelli's flute sonatas Opus II are also in the surviving collection. In general, most of the *musicalia* there has no demonstrable connection with Unico Wilhelm,[83] though his name does appear in the list of subscribers to an edition of 'XXIV Contredances avec leur explication... dedié à... Princesse Caroline d'Orange & Nassau... (Den Haag, n.d.)', which contains dance directions by the court dancing master Gautier with music by N. Deffonesca.[84]

As composer, Unico Wilhelm can be associated with only two of the manuscripts, that of the *Concerti armonici*[85] and of a motet. In the former, the music notations are in another hand – perhaps that of Ricciotti – while the preamble and a number of important annotations, of which more later, are in Unico Wilhelm's own hand. For those who argue that identification on the grounds of hand is, in principle, no less speculative than identification on musical stylistic grounds, other evidence already presented is here repeated in brief: 1) Unico Wilhelm, graaf van Wassenaer amply fulfilled the *Illustre* requirement in the dedication, 2) he was a close friend of Bentinck at the time of publication, 3) he is known to have been obsessed with musical composition in the decade and a half before the publication, 4) the manuscript score with his own annotations has been preserved in the library of his own Castle of Twickel, where many other specimens of his handwriting are also preserved.[86] It seems without question that Unico Wilhelm graaf van Wassenaer is indeed the creator of the *Concerti armonici*.

The second manuscript in the library of Twickel is a motet *Laudate Dominum in sanctis ejus* for two sopranos, bass and *basso continuo*. No composer's name is given, and it is not possible to establish with certainty that handwriting and music hand are those of Unico Wilhelm. Nevertheless, with certain reservations its composition may be ascribed to him on the following grounds. In the first place, it has been preserved in his own library. In the second, a note containing psalm citations from Calmet[87], indisputably written in his own hand, was tucked inside it (see *plate 15*). These citations are 'motet-like' and imply that he had been pre-occupied with compositions of motet structure. These 'external' philological criteria merely point in the direction of Unico Wilhelm van Wassenaer. Stylistic criteria suggest that it was possibly written in his youth, certainly earlier than the *Concerti armonici*. There is some clumsy vocal writing, even consecutive 5ths and octaves (*e.g.* bar 269). Structurally, it is a motet, each section of text having its own musical setting in a different time, tempo or texture from the previous one, and it calls to mind French motets of the first decade of the 18th century,[88] especially those of Campra. Despite its derivative style and sometimes defective technique, it is an agreable-sounding piece, in which one can perhaps hear a presage (bar 369 onwards) of the contrapuntal mastery of the *Concerti armonici*.

The hope that further compositions by the same hand might come to light has not yet been fulfilled. One can speculate with anguish on what the 'groot Paquet zo geschreeve als gedrukt Musicq' which was No. 44 in the sale of books and music, may have contained. Perhaps too much should not be expected quantatively from one who apparently composed the *Concerti armonici* over a space of fifteen years and in later life never had time to make corrections which he himself indicated in the manuscript score.[89]


It is not a simple matter to 'fit' the *Concerti armonici* into any recognised stylistic tradition, Netherlandish or otherwise, particularly in view of the fact that as a composer, Unico Wilhelm van Wassenaer was without doubt a 'cat who walked by himself' and was therefore unrepresentative. At that time, professional composers had to fulfill the requirements of aristocratic or ecclesiastical patrons and the theory that 'independant operators' were more likely to be original seems to be justified by the works of musicians like Gesualdo, Bardi, and even Locatelli, to some extent.[90]

The highly original *Concerti armonici* are not concerti grossi or concertos for four part string orchestra and three solo instruments of a style then customary;[91] they are true seven-voiced

15. Psalm texts in the hand of Count Unico Wilhelm van Wassenaer.

structures.[92] The *violoncello obligato* does not always operate independantly from the bass, but though *colla parte* sections for first and third and/or second and fourth violins do occur, in the main there are four distinct violin lines. There are, however, some unusual factors; for example, the intense, cantabile cello melody set over a rhythmic-melodic *ostinato* in the 3rd movement of the 1st concerto, whose expressiveness is hardly matched in any music of that time. Stylistically, these concertos are in the late baroque tradition, their sonorous effects being achieved by contrapuntal means. In the years between 1725 and 1740, this could not have been regarded as 'progressive', however neutrally that word may be interpreted. (It is, however, worth bearing in mind that at precisely the time when fundamentally new styles were being forged by the Mannheim school, Bach was writing the *Art of Fugue.*) No trace of the roccoco or the galant can be heard in these works. A uniform, sequentially-developed rhythmic-melodic line and often a free contrapuntal linaer concept, or even fugue and fugato, determine the overall structures.

Extraordinarily different hypotheses have been proposed over the past 150 years in the course of attempts to solve the problem of the 'stylistic inexplicability' of the *Concerti armonici*. As far as the Netherlands is concerned, it is certain that late baroque Italian intrumental music figured largely in educated music-making. Unico Wilhelm's library contained the newest publications of Italian string music and the styles of concerto grosso and sonata, *chiesa* and *camera* elements and the niceties of learned counterpoint were obviously familiar to him. Though he cannot have escaped the fascination of the works of Arcangelo Corelli, particularly in Italy during his Grand Tour, it would be an exaggeration to assign the *Concerti armonici* to the *scuola corelliana*, however one may define it.[93] Nevertheless, it is with Corelli that Unico Wilhelm van Wassenaer has some resemblance (one cannot put it as more than that) in consious restraint in the use of stylistic and technical devices, and in a general sense of balance and refinement of sonority. In this connection, Unico Wilhelm's self-critical annotations ('du passable, mediocre et du mauvais' *etc.*) are most revealing. Comments in other parts of the manuscript give evidence of his feeling for balance and propriety. Of the 3rd movement of the 1st concerto (marked *Grave* in the Pergolesi *Collected Edition*, but *Un poco andante* in the manuscript) he wrote 'Ce morceau est un peu trop long' (p.11). He wrote of the last movement of the 2nd concerto 'L'allegro suivant est trop uniforme' (p.35) and of the 3rd movement of the 4th concerto 'un peu trop long'. There is only one instance of a technical comment, again in the 3rd movement of the 4th concerto: 'quelques passages du $1^r$ violon sont un peu forcez pour la main, et auraient besoin d'etre corrigez' (p.74). He noted by the 5th concerto 'Je prefere en tout ce concert a tous les autres' (p.86). Such personal evaluation must be unique for the time.

There is an important note by the fugue in the 2nd movement of the 3rd concerto: 'Le fameux canon qui fait le debut de la fugue suivante n'est pas de Palestrina mais du maître de chapelle de Henri 8 Roy d'Angleterre. On m'a assuré qu'il est gravé sur une plaque de cuivre dans l'eglise de Westminster. Je l'ai mis en concert a la priere d'un amy et j'ai taché, de la remplir dans le meme style. Le canon meme est a 4 parties, et se borne aux 21 premieres mesures'. The name Palestrina, mentioned also in Ricciotti's edition of 1740, is crossed out in the Twickel manuscript. This canon is indeed not the work of Palestrina,[94] but is equally not to be found in the works of Henry VIII's musicians, Fairfax, for example. And it is not graven on a copper plate in Westminster Abbey[95] though it is said to be on a gold plate in the Vatican.[96] Written to the text of Psalm 113, *Non nobis Domine*, it has been ascribed, on rather unsecure grounds, to William Byrd.[97] It was well-known internationally (Mattheson mentioned it in his *Vollkommener Capelmeister*[98] while Corelli[99], Pergolesi[100], Bach[101], Mozart[102] and even Beethoven employed it in theory or composition), but was especially popular in England, where members of the *Academy of Ancient Music* sang it at the end of their meetings.[103] Was it Agostino Steffani, who had contacts in London, who suggested it to Unico Wilhelm, or perhaps Willem Bentinck?

Unico Wilhelm's mastery as a composer has been acknowledged in this century by another composer of genius; Stravinsky based the *Tarantella* in *Pulcinella* entirely on the last movement of the 2nd of the *Concerti armonici*. Musicologists, too, have recognised their great beauty. 'I know of no other Italian concertos of the time which have quite the same dignity and restraint, nor such astonishing beauty in the slow movements. Whoever wrote them was a master, but at the moment I feel we must leave these beautiful concertos attributed to that most prolific of all composers, Signor Anonimo. Yet I would not be in the least surprised any day to hear that they have been found in some

Italian Library bearing the name of an otherwise unknown nobleman', wrote Charles Cudworth, the discoverer of the Pergolesi-Ricciotti connection.[104] This *Signor Anonimo* is now revealed as *Signor Olandese*, a Netherlander whose work lay unrecognised in his own library in his own country for two and a half centuries.

Unico Wilhelm, graaf van Wassenaer is a strong musical personality, the strongest of those born within the present boundaries of the Netherlands since Jacob Obrecht ( † 1505) and Jan Pieterszoon Sweelinck ( † 1621). However one may evaluate Netherlandish composers who came after him, one fact is certain; the music of no other Netherlander has been so esteemed over so long a time by both scholars and music-lovers. Formerly, I had been of the opinion that the great days of musical discovery were virtually over. This find, however, should put new heart into those involved in the study of the musical past of the Netherlands: there is much to be done and, maybe, more to be discovered.

# NOTES

1. See Heinrich Hüschen, article 'Anonymi', in: *Die Musik in Geschichte und Gegenwart*, Vol.I, col.492 *etc.*; Heinrich Kühn, article 'Anonymus', in: *Riemann Musiklexikon*, Sachteil, ed. Hans Heinrich Eggebrecht, Mainz 1967, p.38 *etc.*

2. Jens Peter Larsen, *Die Haydn-Überlieferung*, Kopenhagen 1939, is of fundamental importance in this connection. See also the same author's 'Über die Möglichkeiten einer musikalischen Echtheitsbestimmung für Werke aus der Zeit Haydns und Mozarts', in: *Mozart-Jahrbuch 1971/72* (Salzburg 1973), p.7 *etc.*

3. There is abundant literature on this subject; see the essays in *Authentication in the Visual Arts*, ed. by H.L.C.Jaffé, J.Storm van Leeuwen & L.H.van der Tweel, Amsterdam 1979 and the literature cited there.

4. There is a copy of this edition in the Library of the *Rijksuniversiteit* in Leiden. It is dated by the date of the request for a licence-to-print (26.2.1740); Den Haag, *Algemeen Rijksarchief*, Archief van de Staten van Holland en West-Friesland, inv. no.1694.

5. The original Dutch advertisement reads: 'M$^r$ Sieber, Casteleyn van 't Nieuwe-Vaux-Hall adverteert, dat hij zijn Concerten volgens gewoonte continueert op Dinsdag, Donderdag en Saturdag en dat de Heer Groneman, Directeur van het Muziek van 't Nieuwe Vaux-Hall, op verzoek van zekere Heeren en Liefhebbers, zal laeten executeeren 1 verscheyde extra fraeye Concerten onder andere eenige Concerti Armonici gecomponeerd door een voornaam Heer en gedrukt door C.Ricciotti, detto Batticcia.'

6. See J.Fransen, *Les comédiens français en Hollande au XVIIe et au XVIIIe siècles*, Paris 1925, p.209. Further evidence about Ricciotti in Albert Dunning, 'Zur Frage der Autorschaft der Ricciotti und Pergolesi zugeschriebenen *Concerti armonici*', in: *Anzeiger der phil.-hist. Klasse der Österreichischen Akademie der Wissenschaften*, 1963, p.147 (= *Mitteilungen der Kommission für Musikforschung*, Nr.15); Monique de Smet, *La musique à la cour de Guillaume V, prince d'Orange*, Utrecht 1973, pp.4 and 236 (= *Muziekhistorische Monografieën*, Vol.IV).

7. A copy of this edition is in the Institute of Musicology of the University of Utrecht. For the dating of this reprint, see William C.Smith & Charles Humphries, *A Bibliography of the Musical Works Published by the Firm of John Walsh during the Years 1721-1766*, London 1968, p.286. There is also a second edition by Johnson (see: *Répertoire International des Sources Musicales*). In Johnson's edition, Ricciotti still appears as the dedicator.

8. Johann Philipp Hinnental, 'Zum Problem der Autorschaft der Pergolesi sugeschriebenen Concertini', in: *Die Musikforschung* XXI/3 (1968), p.322 *etc.*

9. I have presented an objection to these views in a short contribution 'Ricciotti und die Concerti armonici, Eine Erwiderung', in: *Die Musikforschung* XXII/3, p.343 *etc.*

10. Nicolaas Selhof, *Catalogue d'une très belle bibliothèque de livres de musique... lesquels seront vendus publiquement aux plus offrans... dans la maison de la veuve d'Adrien Moetjens*, Den Haag 1759, p.164 (reprint in the series *Auction Catalogues of Music*, Amsterdam 1973).

11. Some sections of the *Concerti armonici* were published in *The Musical Antiquarian Magazine. A Collection of Choice Movements from the Ancient Masters*, Arranged, and Edited for Pianoforte, Organ, or Harmonium by Josiah Pittman, London n.d.

12. William Crotch, *Specimens of Various Styles of Music*, London n.d. (ca.1822), Vol.III, p.II. The *Concerto armonici* in B$^\flat$ appears in this collection in a keyboard arrangement.

13. M712.A2 P44.

14. The word 'Concertini' is small, and written in pale ink. It appears to be a later addition.

15. The last line is written in the same way as the word 'Concertini' (see *note 14*) and is probably also a later addition.

16. See Jerzy Morawski, article 'Lessel', in: *Die Musik in Geschichte und Gegenwart*, Vol.VIII, col.668 *etc.*

17. See Karl Gustav Fellerer, article 'Commer', in: *Die Musik in Geschichte und Gegenwart*, Vol.II, col.1583 *etc.*

18. D 12539. The text of the titlepage reads: '6/ Concertini/Per 4 Violoni, Alto, Violoncello/e/Basse continuo/in partizione/del/Pergolesi'. In my article 'Zur Frage der Autorschaft...' (see *note 6*), p.115, I stated incorrectly that this manuscript had once belonged to Franz Commer. This was not so.

19. This information was received from Hans Hoesch (letter dated 31.XII.1962).

20. *Hortus musicus* 150, 82, 159, 144, 154, 155, ed. J.Ph.Hinnental, Kassel 1951-1959, Bärenreiter-Verlag;

*Sei Concertini per Stromenti ad Arco*, ed. F.Caffarelli, Rome 1940, 'Gli amici della musica da camera'; *Concertini Nr.4* (f-minor), ed. San Franko, New York n.d., Schirmer; in the series *Collegium musicum italicum*, edited by Renato Fasano, the *Concertini in G* (no. 1) *and E* , Milan 1959 and 1961, Ricordi: *Concertini No.3 en La Majeur arrangé pour orchestre à cordes avec orgue (ad libitum)*, par Ernest Ansermet, Geneva 1944, Henn.

21. See Charles L.Cudworth, 'Notes on the Instrumental Works attributed to Pergolesi', in: *Music & Letters* XXX (1949), p.321 *etc.*; Frank Walker, 'Two Centuries of Pergolesi Forgeries and Misattributions, in: *Music & Letters* XXXII (1951), p.295 *etc.*; Charles L.Cudworth, 'Pergolesi, Ricciotti, and the Count of Bentinck', in: *Kongress-Bericht der Internationalen Gesellschaft für Musikwissenschaft, Utrecht 1952*, Amsterdam 1953, p.127 *etc.*; Marvin E.Paymer, *Giovanni Battista Pergolesi, 1710-1736. A Thematic Catalogue of the Opera Omnia*, New York 1977, p.9 *etc.*

22. 'Die Zukunft der deutschen Musikforschung', in: *Die Musikforschung* XII (1959), p.173.

23. See François Lesure, *Bibliographie des éditions musicales publiées par Estienne Roger et Michel-Charles le Cène*, Paris 1969.

24. See Albert Dunning, 'Zur Frage der Autorschaft...' (see *note 6*), p.113 *etc.* In my answer to Hinnental's article (see *note 9*) I had already, to some extent, withdrawn my earlier hypothesis. Due to editoral cuts, the methodological framework of my article somewhat fell by the way.

25. In France in December, 1979, I happened to come across a party of Dutch art historians, among them my friend Jacques Vis. In the course of a conversation about the problems of attribution for unsigned and anonymous works, I jokingly defended the thesis that practioners of musicology are a great deal more careful in these matters than commercially-corrupted practioners of art history – a field in which expertise by a 'connoisseur' could raise an object's value far above what it might otherwise have been. In this connection, I cited the case of the authorship of the *Concerti armonici*. Whereupon, one of those present, Wouter van Leeuwen, informed me that in the course of making an inventory of the contents of the Library of a castle in the Netherlands, namely Twickel, he had seen a music manuscript which perhaps – his memory was a little vague – had something to do with this. My surprise at that moment was as great as is my present gratitude to Mr. Van Leeuwen for his information, and for the generous way in which he has since assisted further research in a problem

previously unknown to him as an art historian.

26. For discussion of the character of the manuscript and of the library of Unico Wilhelm, graaf van Wassenaer, see p.21.

27. See H.G.A.Obreen, *De geschiedenis van het geslacht Van Wassenaer*, Leiden 1903.

28. Besides Obreen (see *note 27*, p.147 *etc.*) see *Nederlands Adelsboek*, VI Den Haag 1908, p.539; *ibid*, XXI, Den Haag 1923, p.202 *etc*; *Nieuw Nederlands Biografisch Woordenboek*, ed. P.C.Molhuysen, P.J.Blok and F.K.H. Kossmann, Amsterdam 1974, II, col.1523 *etc.* and col.1540 *etc.*; A.J.van der Aa, *Biografisch woordenboek der Nederlanden*, Haarlem 1877, XX, p.69.

29. See Otto Schutte, *Repertorium der Nederlandse vertegenwoordigers residerende in het buitenland, 1584-1810*, Den Haag, p.208. J.L.van der Klooster, of the *Rijksbureau voor Kunsthistorische Documentatie* in Den Haag, told me of the existence of letters from Unico's father, dating from these periods as ambassador, which are now in the *Algemeen Rijksarchief* (Heinsius-archief) in Den Haag, in the family archives at Twickel and in the *Koninklijke Bibliotheek* in Den Haag. Without the generous help of Mr. L.J.van der Klooster this biography of Unico Wilhelm would have been much less complete. I am indebted to him for the content of footnotes 30, 32, 33, 35, 36, 37, 39, 40 en 42, which I hereby acknowledge, and for many references from letters and documents in the family archives from Castle Twickel, which have been known to him for at least twenty years. At present (1980) these records are in the *Rijksarchief* in Zwolle for classification and cataloguing. Thanks to the Twickel Foundation it is expected that they will ultimately be returned to the Castle. This new catalogue will supersede the old and very rudimentary listing.

30. E.g. Otto Schutte, (see *note 29*), p.208.

31. Further information about music at the court in Düsseldorf can be found in Alfred Einstein, 'Italienische Musiker am Hofe der Neuburger Wittelsbacher', in: *Sammelbände der Internationalen Musikgesellschaft* IX (1907/ 1908), p.336 *etc.*; Fritz Zobeley, 'Zur Hofmusik des Kurfürsten Johann Wilhelm', in: *Beiträge zur Musikgeschichte der Stadt Düsseldorf*, ed. Karl-Gustav Fellerer, Krefeld 1952, p.9 *etc.* (= *Beiträge zur rheinischen Musikgeschichte*, Vol.I); Gerhard Steffen, *Johann Hugo von Wilderer (1670 bis 1724), Kapellmeister am kurpfälzischen Hofe zu Düsseldorf und Mannheim*, Cologne 1960 (= *Beiträge zur rheinischen Musikgeschichte*, Vol.XL): Wolf-dieter Meinardus, article 'Düsseldorf', in: *Die Musik in Geschichte und Gegenwart*, Vol.III, col.870 *etc.*

32. See D.P.M.Graswinkel, 'Het Paleis Kneuterdijk', in: *Die Haghe. Jaarboek 1937*, p.23 *etc.* The house designed in 1723 by Marot, for Unico's brother Johan Hendrik, was on this site. See p.18.

33. Den Haag, *Gemeente-archief*, Records of the Walloon Church, No. 101.

34. *Album studiosorum Academiae Lugduno Batavae, MDLXXV-MDCCCLXXV*, Den Haag 1875, col.818.

35. Letter from Carrier to Unico's father (formerly in the folder for 1688-1713, Twickel).

36. Correspondence of Unico's father; family archives from Twickel.

37. Den Haag, *Algemeen Rijksarchief*, Archief Staten van Holland.

38. Den Haag, *Algemeen Rijksarchief*, Archief van de Staten-Generaal, No.8667; see also G.J. ter Kuile, *Geschiedkundige aantekeningen op de havezathen van Twenthe*, Almelo 1911, pp.226 and 236.

39. See G.J.ter Kuile, (see *note 38*), p.226.

40. Den Haag, *Algemeen Rijksarchief*, Provinciale Resoluties (Overijssel), No.494-495. See also J.van Doorninck, *Geslachtkundige aantekeningen ten aanzien van de gecommitteerden ten landdage van Overijssel*, Deventer 1871, p.282 *etc.*

41. See *note 39*.

42. Copy of a letter from Unico Wilhelm to Corsini; family archives Twickel.

43. This letter is now filed with the personal papers of Johan Hendrik.

44. For further information about Willem Bentinck see Willemina Catharina van Huffel, *Willem Bentinck van Rhoon. Zijn persoonlijkheid en leven 1725-1757*, Den Haag 1923; Antoine Jean d'Ailly, *Willem Bentinck van Rhoon en de diplomatieke betrekkingen tusschen Engeland en de Nederlandse Republiek gedurende de laatste jaren voor de Vrede van Aken in 1748*, Amsterdam 1898; C.Gerretson and P.Geyl, *Briefwisseling en aantekeningen van Willem Bentinck, Heer van Rhoon*, Utrecht 1934, Bd.I.

45. P.Geyl, 'Een opvoeding in de achttiende eeuw', in: *Bijdragen voor vaderlandsche Geschiedenis en Oudheidkunde*, 5de reeks, Vol.9, p.233 *etc.* gives an insight into specific aspects of this guardianship.

46. Preserved in the Castle of Twickel and (in great quantity) in the Egerton Collection in the *British Library*, London; Th.Bussemaker gave a description of the latter, in: *Bijdragen en Mededelingen van het Historisch Genootschap*, XXVIII (1907), p.XL *etc.* These letters were drawn on by Hella Haase, whose lively and fascinating book *Mevrouw Bentinck of Onverenigbaarheid van karakter*, Amsterdam 1978, tells the story of the wrecked marriage between Willem Bentinck and Charlotte Sophie, Countess of Aldenburg.

47. Letter from Johan Hendrik, graaf van Wassenaer, dated 17.11.1722, to the Duchess of Portland; London, *British Library*, Egerton 1711, fol.92-95.

48. See London, *British Library*, Egerton 1711, fol.234. In Albert Dunning, 'Zur Frage der Autorschaft...' (see *note 6*), p.119 the 'Blankenbourg' in this letter was incorrectly thought to be a music-dealer. This bill must relate to Bentinck's harpsichord-teacher Quirinus van Blankenburg. See also *Egerton 1711*, fol.234 *etc* and fol.281 *etc.* containing respectively bills for 5.11.1726 and 3.5.1726.

49. Letter from Willem Bentinck to the Duchess of Portland (uncertain date, probably 1723); London, *British Library*, Egerton 1711, fol.151.

50. A summary is in Albert Dunning (see *note 6*), p.119-120.

51. Sei Sonate/a Tre/Due Violini & Violoncello ò Basso Continuo.../Opera prima/gravé par Alexis Magito Fils/A Rotterdam' In A. Dunning, (see *note 6*), p.120 it is incorrectly suggested that Willem Bentinck must have been the dedicatee. The name of Alexis Magito appears also on the last plate of the first violin part of the *Concerti armonici*.

52. *Livre de clavecin et d'orgues*, Den Haag 1745. I am indebted for this information to the Utrecht student Job de Ruiter, who is currently preparing a detailed study of Van Blankenburg. I am also grateful for his help in preparing this publication for the press.

53. *Six symphonies... opera seconda*, Amsterdam ca.1770, J.J.Hummel. For Ricci's connections with the court in Den Haag, see Monique de Smet, *La musique à la cour de Guillaume V, prince d'Orange (1748-1806)*, Utrecht 1973, (= *Muziekhistorische Monografieën*, Vol.4).

54. See W.A. Mozart, *Briefe und Aufzeichnungen, Gesamtausgabe*, ed. William A.Bauer and Otto Erich Deutsch, Kassel-Basel-London-New York 1962, Vol.I p.216.

55. London, *British Library*, Egerton 1711, fol.239-240.

56. A letter from Bernège to the Duchess of Portland, dated 30.11.1725, in London, *British Library*, Egerton 1711, fol.196. Bernège described a domestic concert at Mons.ʳ de Twickle's house at which 'un prince Moscovite' was present, and on fol.244 there is mention of a concert there 'qui dura jusqu'à dix heures du soir'. According to a letter of 5.3.1726 from Bernège to the Duchess of Portland (Egerton 1711, fol.215) the French ambassador Fénelon and the Prince of Nassau-Siegen and 'Boetselaar

le Capitain' were present at a concert in Bentinck's house.

57. *E.g.* P.Geyl (see *note 45*).

58. See J.Fransen (see *note 6*).

59. London, *British Library*, Egerton 1711, fol.1723 (letter from Willem Bentinck to the Duchess of Portland, dated 15.2.1723).

60. London, *British Library*, Egerton 1711, fol.613.

61. Many letters from Bentinck to Unico Wilhelm van Wassenaer-Twickel and vice versa are preserved in the Egerton collection in the British Library. They deal mostly with official business, but there are some personal exchanges: Egerton 1745, fol.120, Bentinck (18.3.1746) to Unico Wilhelm: 'j'attends de vous que comme nous avons toujours pris nos mesures ensemble dans d'autres qualités, nous continuerons sur le même pied dans les nouvelles relations que nous avons ensembles'; answer from Unico Wilhelm in Versailles, dated 25.3.1746 (Egerton 1745): 'et vous pouvez comptez que je ne ferai jamais rien, que préalablement je n'en aye concerté avec vous. Nous ne serons pas toujours de même avis, mais tout s'arrange. Il est certain que j'ay resolu de très bonne foy, de contribuer de tout mon pouvoir à nourir l'union et la confiance entre vous et moy... Je vous embrasse de grand cœur'; Bentinck to Unico Wilhelm, dated 14.3.1747 (Egerton 1745, fol.163): 'Je vous donne connoissance comme à un ancien amy de moi et des miens...'. The Egerton letters from 1745, fol.164 and 623, and from 1748, fol.261 provide little that is relevant to our investigation. In No.658 of the Bentinck records, formerly in Middachten, now in the *Rijksarchief* in Arnhem, Unico Wilhelm wrote to Willem Bentinck on 8.5.1750, informing him of the death of his sister Amadea: 'Les relations qui ont subsisté entre vous et ma famille m'imposent le devoir de vous faire part de la perte sensible que je viens de faire d'une sœur... Vous avez connu de tout tems son amitié pour vous; ce n'est pas sans peine qu'elle s'étoit aperçue que depuis quelque tems il y a eu de l'alteration dans vos sentiments.'

62. *E.g.* in Gerretson and Geyl's edition of Bentinck's letters cited in *note 44*. See also Th. Bussemaker, 'Uittreksels uit de brieven van d'Affry aan de Fransche Regering', in: *Bijdragen en Mededelingen van het Historisch Genootschap* XXVII (1906), p.312.

63. Zwolle, *Rijksarchief*, Family records from Twickel, provisional No. 247.

64. See H.G.A.Obreen, (see *note 27*), p.147.

65. See H.G.A.Obreen, (see *note 27*), p.147-148.

66. This is L.J. van der Klooster's opinion.

67. *Algemeen Nederlandsch Familieblad*, No.62, 22 November 1883, p.5.

68. L.J.van der Klooster, Daniel Marot en de Graaf van Wassenaer-Obdam. Rondom een brief uit 1711', in: *Bulletin van de Koninklijke Nederlandse Oudheidkundige Bond*, 74 (1975), p.135-143. See also M.D.Ozinga, *Daniël Marot, de schepper van den Hollandschen Lodewijk XIV$^{de}$-stijl*, Amsterdam 1938.

69. *E.g.* Otto Schutte, (see *note 29*), p.142.

70. Besides the literature already cited, see T.Jorissen, 'Lord Chesterfield en de Republiek der Vereenigde Nederlanden', in: *Historische Studiën*, Haarlem 1894, Vol.V; *Archives ou correspondence inédites de la Maison d'Orange-Nassau*, Quatrième série, publiée par Th.Bussemaker, Tome I, II, III, IV et Suppl., Leiden 1908-1914; A.Beer, *Holland und der Österreichische Erbfolgekrieg*, Vienna 1871.

71. From this painting J.A.Boland made an engraving which is reproduced in P.Verloren van Themaat, *Archieven der Ridderlijke Duitse Orde, Balie van Utrecht*, Utrecht 1871, Vol.I, No.XLVI. The portrait itself has been reproduced in E.Pelinck, Joan van Gybelant, Schout en baljuw van Wassenaer en Zuidwijk', in: *Jaarboekje voor Geschiedenis en Oudheidkunde van Leiden en omstreken*, LIV (1962), p.85 *etc.*

72. This identification has been made by J.L.van der Klooster. The subject was formerly thought to have been Unico's brother, Johan Hendrik graaf van Wassenaer-Obdam.

73. Houbraken's engraving can be found in J.Wagenaar, *Vaderlandsche Historie*, Vol.XX, Amsterdam 1759, between p.22 and 23.

74. *E.g.* acquaintance with men like Neri Corsini (born in 1685 in Florence, representative of Cosimo III de' Medici in Den Haag, London and Paris), cardinal from 1730. For discussion of Corsini as patron see Ludwig von Pastor, *Geschichte der Päpste seit dem Ausgang des Mittelalters*, Freiburg-in-Breisgau $^7$1930, Vol.XV.

75. The *Cantus, Bassus* and *Quintus* part-books of this work are in the Twickel library. For the dedication, see Alfons Annegarn, *Floris en Cornelis Schuyt*, Utrecht 1973, p.135 *etc.* (= *Muziekhistorische Monografieën*, Vol.V).

76. *Catalogue d'une bibliothèque... ainsi qu'une collection de musique... receuillie... par... Messire Jacob Jan, Comte & Seigneur Banneret de Wassenaer... lesquels seront vendus publiquement... le Mardi 9 Decembre 1788... par Pierre Fréderic Gosse... A La Haye.* A copy of this catalogue is in the Royal Library in Den Haag, No.4447. A few other musical items appear on pages other than those reproduced in this volume; For example 'Un Paquet de Tragédies, Comé-

dies Comiques ʃrançois & Italien' on p.171.

77. The publication dates of the works offered for sale in this catalogue strongly suggest that most of them had been Unico Wilhelm's property. (This does not apply to Nos. 33-42).

78. Hella Haase (see *note 46*).

79. My uncovering of these works in the library of the Castle of Twickel was consequent upon information provided by Wouter van Leeuwen, for which I am deeply grateful.

80. Opus I, Amsterdam (ca. 1739), Witvogel. Opus II, also printed by Witvogel is a unique copy (see Albert Dunning, *De muziekuitgever Gerhard Fredrik Witvogel en zijn fonds*, Utrecht 1966, p.52). The text of the title page reads: *VI SONATE/A VIOLINO SOLO/CON CEMBALO OVERO BASSO DI VIOLA/DEDICATE/ALLA SUBLIMA INTELLIGENZA/DI/SUA ALTEZZA REALE/PRINCIPESSA D'ORANGE E DI NASSAU/&c. &c. &c./OPERA SECONDA/DA FRANCESCO GUERINI NAPOLITANO/MUSICO DI CAMERA, ALL' ATTUALE SERVITIO/DI DETTA SUA ALTEZZA REALE/ STAMPATE A SPESE/DI GERHARDO FREDERICO WITVOGEL/ORGANISTA DELLA CHIESA NUOVA LUTERANA/ A AMSTERDAM/No.81.* There is one more set of violin duets by Guerini, Opus V, Den Haag, chez l'auteur, and Amsterdam J.J.Hummel. The Twickel library also possesses a copy of Witvogel's *Zangwysen* (No.2). This copy has many handwritten corrections and additions and was perhaps the source of the second edition by Covens: (this has not been checked).

81. This copy carries the signature of C.Bentinck, presumably Willem's brother Charles, a member of Unico Wilhelm's music-making circle in Den Haag. The same signature appears on the British Library's copy of Ricciotti's edition of the *Concerti armonici*.

82. The name St.Auban, *i.e.* Guido Pape, Marquis of St.Auban, who was married to Unico Wilhelm's sister, and was among those who took part in the domestic music-making in the houses of Willem Bentinck and M^r de Twickle, is on this copy.

83. Titles include: Cammerloher, *VI Sinfonie... opera seconda*, Liège; *Livre septième des chansons vulgaires*, Amsterdam 1632, (= RISM 16325: only *superius*); several printed part books with works by Peter Philips, Orologio, Dentice, R.Giovanelli, del Mel, Vecchi, Striggio and Belli; whether these are the residue of a working music-library used by the family in the 17th century, or were bought long after publication as antiquarian pieces is now

difficult to establish. Also, a manuscript '*Clavierboek van Zuiryn van Bambeek van Strijen, Anno 1752*' containing works by Hurlebusch, Chelleri, Venturini, Handel, Hasse and Alberti.

84. Among the family records from Twickel there is a manuscript copy of an air *Dépit mortel transport*, which is certainly in Unico Wilhelm's hand, stored in a folder with items relating to the *Orde van Tombago* (see *note 63*). I have been able to identify the air as coming from Lully's *Thésée* (see Lully, *Receuil des plus beaux endroits des operas*, Paris n.d., Vol.I, p.58^v).

85. Though the title *Concerti armonici* does not appear in this manuscript, it seams reasonable to retain it for these concertos, since it is unquestionable that Ricciotti's publication in which they were so named was made in close co-operation with Unico Wilhelm.

86. L.J.van der Klooster, (see *note 68*), p.137.

87. '*Extraits de Psaumes. Calmet, T.II*': Ps.149,1; Ps.116, 5; Ps.117,2; Ps.118,14; Ps.17; Ps.114,1,4. See Augustin Calmet, *Dissertations sur la poésie et la musique des Anciens...*, Tome premier, seconde partie, Amsterdam 1723.

88. The possibility that this might be a motet of French provenance was largely ruled out by research into French motets of the first half of the 18th century, in the course of which I consulted the catalogue of text incipits in the *Bibliothèque Nationale*, Paris.

89. Several years ago, I found an anonymous collection of violin sonatas from the year 1735 (*XII SONATE /A VIOLINO VIOLONCELLO O CIMBALO/DEDICATE ALLA SERENISSIMA ALTEZZA REALE/LA PRINCIPESSA/ANNA ORANGES &&&/DA/N.N./ OPERA PRIMA/A L'HAIJA*) in the Castle of Leufsta in Sweden (see Albert Dunning, 'Die De Geerschen Musikalien in Leufsta. Musikalische schwedish-niederländische Beziehungen im 18. Jh.', in: *Svensk Tidskrift för Musikforskning* XLVII (1966), p.187 *etc.*) The dedication gives no further information as to who could have offered these works anonymously to Anna, the wife of the *Stadhouder* of Friesland, Groningen en Gelderland, herself a musician and one-time pupil of Handel. Whoever the composer was (untraceable Pasterus, according to the Leufsta copy?), it cannot have been Unico Wilhelm. These sonatas are well-contrived for the violin, but in their quick movements, (here and there already *galant* in style) there is a lack of the thematic energy so characteristic of the *Concerti armonici*, while the slow movements are colourless and uninspired. One may agree with Horace that '*aliquando dormitat et bonus Homerus*'; nevertheless, on grounds of method and style these cannot

be attributed to Unico Wilhelm. No trace of the master hand which is on every page of the *Concerti armonici* can be found in these pieces; and though genius may nod, it does not do so for the length of 12 entire sonatas.

90. See A. Dunning, *Pietro Antonio Locatelli, 1695-1764. Der Virtuose und seine Welt*, Buren 1981 (in the press).

91. Charles Avison and Michel Festing (both of them pupils of Geminiani) wrote concertos in 'seven parts'. I have not seen scores of these works and therefore cannot assess what, if anything, they may have in common with the *Concerti armonici*. They are probably ordinary concerti grossi.

92. There are occasional solo passages, for example in the third movement of *Concerto armonico* in G, No.4, which are not marked in the manuscript score from Twickel but are present in Ricciotti's edition of 1740 and therefore also in the Pergolesi *Collected Edition* which was taken from Ricciotti. These passages, however, do not change the pieces into solo concertos, or concertos for several solo instruments. These subtle additions must have had the composer's approval, since Ricciotti, as director of Unico Wilhelm's group of performers, must have been familiar with the way they were actually performed.
The concerto numbering used in this study follows that in the manuscript from the Castle of Twickel. The various manuscript and printed sources are numbered as follows:
Ms.Twickel; Ricciotti edition 1740; Walsh edition 1755:
1, 2, 3, 4, 5, 6
Mss. Washington, Paris, Hoesch; Pergolesi, *Opera-Omnia*:
1, 6, 3, 2, 4, 5

93. As does Francesco Degrada in his remarkably well-documented article 'Le messe di Giovanni Battista Pergolesi. Problemi di cronologia e d'attribuzione', in: *Analecta Musicologica* III (1966), p.67.
Further information about followers of Corelli (or a 'Corelli-school') can be found in the references cited in Dunning 1981 (see *note 90*), Book I, Chapter 3.

94. Not included in Joh.Jac.Adr.van der Walt, *Die Kanongestaltung im Werk Palestrinas*, Cologne 1956, or in Haberl's *Palestrina-Gesamtausgabe*.

95. Written communication dated 1.VI.1980 from Howard M.Nixon, librarian of the Muniment Room and Library of Westminster Abbey, London.

96. See W.S.Rockstro, article 'Non nobis Domine', in: *Grove's Dictionary of Music and Musicians*, London [5]1954, p.99. I have not pursued this subject further.

97. William Byrd, *Collected Vocal Works*, ed. Edmund H.Fellowes, London 1948, Vol.XVI, p.106 *etc.* and E.H.Fellowes, *William Byrd*, London 1948, p.178 *etc.*

98. Hamburg 1739, p.409.

99. According to Mario Fabbri, 'Tredici ignote composizioni attribuite a Corelli, in due manoscritte di Firenze e di Assisi', in: *Chiagana* XX (1963), p.23 *etc.*

100. Francesco Degrada, (see *note 93*), p.67.

101. J.S.Bach, *Gesamtausgabe*, Vol.XXXVIII, p.121.

102. KV 6, Anh. A3. See also Warren Kirkendale, *Fugue and Fugato in Rococo and Classical Chamber Music*, Durham N.C. 1979, p.212.

103. According to Carl Ferdinand Pohl, *Mozart und Haydn in London*, Vol.I, Vienna 1867, p.16.

104. See C.Cudworth, (see *note 21*), p.131.

# PART TWO
# FACSIMILES

## 1. MANUSCRIPT OF THE SIX 'CONCERTI ARMONICI'

Partition de mes concerts, gravez
par le Sr. Ricciotti, Surnommé Bachiche.

Ces concerts ont été Composés en diferens tems
entre les années 1725 et 1740.

à mesure qu'ils furent faits, je les portai au concert
Etabli a la Haye, entre Messrs Bentinck, moy, et
quelques seigneurs Etrangers. Ce dit Bachiche y jouait
le 1r violon.; je lui permis d'en prendre successivement
Copie; la demie douzaine, etant complette, il me demanda
permission de les faire graver. Sur mon refus reitere,
il implora le secours de Mrs Bentinck de Roon, sur les
fortes instances duquel, je me rendis enfin, a condition
que mon nom n'y paraitrait points et qu'il pourroit y
mettre le sien, ce qu'il fit : il voulut me le dedier; je le
refusai absolument; Sur quoy Mr Bentinck lui dit de les
luij dedier.
C'est ainsi que ces concerts sont devenus publics, contre
mon intention;
Il y a du passable, du mediocre, du mauvais; sans la publication, j'en aurois, peut etre, corrigé les defauts, mais
d'autres occupations ne m'ont pas laissé le loisir de m'y
amuser; et j'aurois fait tort a l'editeur.

Concerto 2.
Grave
Piano Forte

2
Allegro
tasto solo

10

Un poco andante
staccato sempre
Ce morceau est un peu trop long.

Cantabile

Cantabile

Forte
Allegro

16

17

18

Concerto II
Largo Andante

tasto solo

Tasto Solo
Segue Subito

27
Da Capella. Presto

28

32
tasto solo
adagio
I.
P.
P.
Forte
P.

Largo affettuoso.

34

l'allegro suivant
est trop languissant.

Allegro moderato. Meno forte

tasto solo

Concerto III
Grave. Sostenuto
Le fameux canon qui fait
le debut de la fugue suivante,
n'est pas de Palestrina,
mais du maitre de Chapelle
de Henri 8. Roy d'Angleterre: on m'assure qu'il
est gravé sur une plaque
de Cuivre dans l'eglise de
Westmunster.
j'ai mis en concert
a la priere d'un ami,
et j'ai taché, de le rem=
=plir dans le meme
style.
le canon meme est a
4. parties, et se borne
aux 21. premieres =
mesures.
Da Capella. Canone di Palestrina.

44

45
Tasto solo

48

98
Largo, andante
Affettuoso
P.
P.
P.
P.
F.
F.
F.
F.

52
J.

55.

58
MT.

59
M.f.

Concerto IV.
Largo
Piano.
Forte

Da Capella, non presto

70

74
Le Largo qui
suit est un
peu trop long,
et quelques
passages du
1. violon
sont un peu
forcés pour
la main, et
méritent les
soins d'être
corrigés.

Largo affettuoso

tutti

78
Solo
tutti

80
Allegro.

82

T.1.

86
Concerto
V.
Adagio  1.°  Largo
Je Urefere en tout ce concert a tous les autres.
Segue  Segue

85
[Cassano

Faratgriella

93

94

96
Con sordino

101
a Tempo
Giusto

102

106

Concerto
VI.
Menuose

109

Presto

115.

117
T.S.

116
Largo.

F.ne
Vivace

123

126

# PART TWO
# FACSIMILES

## 2. MANUSCRIPT OF THE MOTET
## 'LAUDATE DOMINUM IN SANCTIS EIUS'

Motet a 2. Dessus et Basse.
vivem:
Laudate Dominum Laudate — Laudate Dominum Lau=
Laudate Dominum lauda te- Laudate Dominum Lau=
Lauda te Dominum lauda-te- Laudate Dominum Lau=
=da -te lauda - te lauda - - - te in sanctis ejus Lau=
=da -te lauda - te Lauda - - te in sanctis ejus Lau=
=da -te Lauda -te lauda - te Dominum in sanctis ejus lauda -
=da -te Lauda - - - - - te Laudate Dominum Lau=
=da -te Lauda - - - te Laudate Dominum Lau=
te Laudate Dominum laudate
=Da - - - te Lauda - - te in sanctis ejus
=da - - - te Lauda - - te in Sanctis ejus Laudate
Laudate Dominum Lauda - - te in sanctis ejus Laudate

Lauda - te Lauda - - - - - - - te Lau=
Dominum laudate Lauda - - - - te Lau=
Domi -num Lauda - - - - te Dominum Lau
Da - - - - - te Laudate Dominum Laudate in Sanctis
Da - - - - te Laudate Dominum Laudate in Sanctis
Da - - - - - te Laudate Dominum in Sanctis
J Dell: Solo.
e -jus. Laudate Deum
e -jus.
e - jus. moder:
in Firmamento virtu-tis e - jus Lauda - - - -

te in firmamento virtutis e - jus
Laudate Laudate
eum in virtutibus ejus Lauda - - - - te in vir=
=tu - - tibus e - jus.
Laudate Lauda - - - te Lau -
=Da - - - - - te e - um secundum -

mul ti -tu dinem magni tu dinis e - jus Laudate eum
secundum mul ti tu dinem magni tu-dinis e - jus magni tu dinis
Laudate Deum in Firmamento virtu- tis ejus Lau=
Lauda - - - te in Firmamento virtu tis-
e - jus Lauda - - - te
Da - - - te eum in virtutibus e -
ejus Laudate eum Lauda - - te eum in virtutibus e -
in Firmamento virtu -tis ejus Lauda te eum in virtutibus e -

=jus Lauda-te eum Secundum multi-tu-dinem magni=
=jus Lauda-te eum Secundum multi tu-dinem magni=
=jus Lauda-te eum Secundum multi-tu-dinem magni=
=tudinis e-jus magni tu dinis e---jus.
=tudinis e-jus magni tu dinis e---jus.
=tu dinis e-jus magni tu dinis e---jus.
a 2. Dessus.
Tact
vivace.
Lauda te Deum Lauda---te Lauda----
Lauda-te Deum Lauda--te Lau=
---te Lauda te Deum in So---no in Sono tu=
=da----te Lauda te Deum in So---no in Sono tu=

bæ Lauda - - - te Lauda - - - -
bæ Lauda - - - te Lauda -
- - - te in So - - - - - - no tuba Lau.
- - - te in So - - - - no tuba
Pate Deum Lauda - - - - te.
Lauda - te Deum Lauda - - te.
Laudate e - um in Psalterio et citha -
ra Lauda te e - um Lauda - - te in Psalte - rio -
et cithara Lauda te eum Lauda - - -
folo
moder:
Tutt.
Spiccato

te in Psalterio
et cithara.
a 3.
vivace.
Lauda te Deum in tijmpano et Choro et Cho-ro Lauda-
Lauda te Deum in tijmpano et Choro et Cho-ro Lauda-
Lauda te Deum in tümpano et Choro et Cho-ro Lau-
te Lauda- te in tijmpano in tijmpano et Cho-
te Lauda- te in tümpano et Cho-
te in tijmpano et-
ro et Cho-ro Lauda- te Lauda-
ro et Choro Lauda- te Lauda-
Cho- ro et Choro Lauda- te Deum Lau-

- te in tijmpano et cho -
- te in Tijmpano et cho -
- Da - - te in tijmpano et cho -
- ro in tijmpano et cho - ro. Lauda -
- ro in tijmpano et cho - ro. Lauda -
- ro et cho - ro. Laudate eum in cijmbalis
affett.
- te eum in cijmbalis bene sonantibus Lauda -
- te eum in cijmbalis bene sonantibus Lauda -
bene sonantibus Lauda te eum Lauda -
- te in cijmbalis jubilati - o - nis Laudate Lau -
- te in cijmbalis jubilati - o - nis Laudate Lau -
- te in cijmbalis jubilati - o - nis Lauda -

vivace
date Lauda - - - - te in cijmbalis jubilati - o - nis.
date Lauda - - - te in cijmbalis jubilati - o - nis.
- te Lauda - - te cum Lauda te in cijmbalis jubilati - o - nis.
vivace
Laudate Deum in tijmpano et Choro et cho-ro Lauda - - te in =
Laudate Deum in tijmpano et Choro et cho-ro Lauda - - te -
Lauda te Deum in tijmpano et Choro et Cho-ro Lauda - -
tijmpano et cho - - - - - ro in tijmpano et cho-ro.
in tijmpano et cho - - - ro in tijmpano et cho-ro.
- te in tijmpano et cho - - ro et cho - - - ro.
Sostenuto Lauda - - - - te Lauda - - te cum Lau =
Lauda - - - - te eum in -
Lauda - - te eum in -

-da - - - - te in Chordis et- orga no Lauda - - - te eum Lauda -
Chordis et organo Lauda - - - - - te eum Lauda - - te
Chordis et organo Lau da - - - te Lauda te eum Lauda - -
- - - - - te in Chordis et - orga -no Lauda - - te eum Lau -
eum Lauda - - - - te in Chordis et orga -no Lauda - - te
- te eum Laudate Lauda - - - te Lauda - - - te eum Lauda te in -
-da - - - - - te in Chordis et organo Lauda - - -
eum Lauda - - - - - - te in Chordis et orga -no Lauda -
Chordis et organo Lauda te eum Lauda - - - te eum Laudate e -
-te Lauda - - - te Lauda - - - - te eum
- - te Lauda - - - - - - te eum Lauda - te Lau -
-um Lauda - - - - te in Chordis et organo Laudate eum Laudate Lauda -

Lauda - - - - - te in chordis et organo Lauda - - -
Da - - - te Lauda te cum in chordis et organo Lauda - - -
- - te in chordis et or - - - gano Lauda te -
- - te in chordis et organo Lauda - te.
- - te in chordis et organo Lauda - te.
cum laudate Lauda - - - - te Lauda - te.
Da capella
Omnis spiritus Lau - - - det Domi
Omnis spiritus Lau - - det laudet Do - minum laudet Domi
Omnis
- num omnis Spiritus Laudet Dominum Lau - - - det Domi -
- num Lau - - det Dominum Lau - - - Det Domi -
spiritus Lau - - - det Dominum Lau - det Laudet Domi -

-num omnis Spiritus Lau - - det Laudet Do - minum.
-num Lau - - det Dominum Lau - - det Dominum
-num Lau - - det Dominum omnis Spiritus Lau - - det Dominum Lau -
Lau - - det Laudet Dominum Lau - - - det omnis Spiritus
Lau - - det Lau - - det Lau - - - det omnis
det Do - minum omnis Spiritus Lau -
Lau - - det Dominum Lau - - det Lau - - det Dominum
Spiritus Laudet Dominum Lau - - - det Lau-det Lau - - det Dominum
-det Laudet Do - mi num Lau - - - det Lau - - - det Dominum
Omnis Spiritus Laudet Lau det Dominum Lau - det Do - minum.
Omnis Spiritus Laudet Dominum Lau - - det Domi num.
Omnis Spiritus Laudet Dominum Lau - - - det Dominum.
Lent:

# PART THREE
# TRANSCRIPTION

MOTET 'LAUDATE DOMINUM IN SANCTIS EIUS'

# LAUDATE DOMINUM IN SANCTIS EIUS

## MOTET FOR TWO SOPRANOS, BASS AND *BASSO CONTINO*

REALISATION OF THE FIGURED BASS BY
ANNEKE UITTENBOSCH

lau-da- -te lau-da- - - - - -te lau-
Do- -mi-num lau- da- -te lau- da- - - - - -te lau-
Do- -mi-num lau- - - - - - -te Do- -mi-num lau-
da- - - - - - -te lau-da-te Do- -mi-num lau- da- -te in sanc- -tis
da- - - - - - -te lau- da-te Do- -mi-num lau da- -te in sanc- -tis
da- - - - - -te lau-da-te Do- -mi-num in sanc- -tis
Moderato
e- -ius
e- -ius
e- -ius
Lau- da- -te De- um in fir- ma- men- -to vir- tu- -tis e-
-ius lau- da-

59
-te in fir- -ma- -men- -to vir- -tu- -tis e- -ius
Lau- da- -te
65
lau- -da- -te e- -um in vir- -tu- -ti- bus e- -ius lau- da-
71
-te in vir- -tu- -ti- bus
77
e- -ius lau- da- -te lau- da- -te lau-
83
da- -te e- -um

se- -cun -dum mul- -ti- -tu- -di- nem mag- ni- -tu- -di- nis e-
-ius lau- -da- -te e- -um se- -cun- -dum mul- -ti- -tu- -di- nem
mag- -ni- -tu- -di- nis e- -ius mag- -ni- -tu- -di- nis e-
Lau- -da- -te De- -um in fir- -ma- -men- -to vir- -tu- -tis
Lau- -da- -te in fir- -ma- -men- -to vir-
Lau- -da-
-ius
e- -ius lau- -da- -te
-tu- -tis e- -ius lau- -da- -te e- -um lau- -da- -te
-te in fir- -ma- -men- -to vir- -tu- -tis e- -ius lau- -da- -te

-no in so- -no tu- -bae lau- da- -te lau- da-
-no in so- -no tu- bae. lau- da- -te lau- da-
5 6
-te in so-
-te in so-
7
-no tu- -bae lau- da- -te De- -um lau- da- -te
-no tu- -bae lau- da- -te De- -um lau- da- -te
Moderato
Lau- da- -te e- -um
spiccato
in psal- -te- -ri- o et ci- tha- ra lau- da- -te e- -um lau-
4
-da- -te in psal- -te- -ri- o et ci- tha- ra
6 8

230
-ro lau- da- -te lau- da- -
-ro lau- da- -te lau- da- -
-ro lau- da- -te De- um lau- da-
7
237
-te in tym- pa- no et cho- -ro in
-te in tym- pa- no et cho- -ro in
-te in tym- pa- no et cho- -ro et
7
244
Affettuoso
tym- pa- no et cho- -ro Lau- da-
tym- pa- no et cho- -ro Lau- da-
cho- -ro Lau- da- -te
6 5 3
4 4
250
-te e- -um in cym- -ba- -lis be- ne so-
-te e- -um in cym- -ba- -lis be- ne so-
e- -um in cym- -ba- lis be- ne so- nan- -ti- bus lau- da- -te e- um lau-
5
256
-nan- -ti- bus lau- da- -te
-nan- -ti- bus lau- da- -te
-da- -te
5 7

in cym- -ba- -lis iu-bi-la-ti- -o- -nis lau- -da- -te
in cym- -ba- -lis iu-bi-la-ti- -o- -nis lau- -da- -te
in cym- -ba- -lis iu-bi-la-ti- -o- -nis lau- -da-
6
5 4 3
lau- -da- -te lau- -da- -te
lau- -da- -te lau- -da- -te
-te lau- -da- -te e- -um lau- -da- -te
5 4 3
in cym- -ba- -lis iu-bi-la-ti- -o- -nis lau-
in cym- -ba- -lis iu-bi-la-ti- -o- -nis lau-
in cym- -ba- -lis iu-bi-la-ti- -o- -nis lau-
Vivace
-cla- -te De- -um in tym- -pa-no et cho- -ro et cho- -ro lau- -da-
-da- -te De- -um in tym- -pa-no et cho- -ro et cho- -ro lau- -da-
-da- -te De- -um in tym- -pa-no et cho- -ro et cho- -ro lau-
-te in tym- -pa-no et cho- -ro in tym- -pa-no et
-te in tym- -pa-no et cho- -ro in tym- -pa-no et
-cla- -te in tym- -pa-no et cho- -ro et cho-
6
4

294
Sostenuto
cho- -ro
cho- -ro
-ro
300
Lau- -da- -te lau- -da-
Lau- -da-
Lau- -da-
306
-te e- -um lau- -da- -te in chor- dis et
-te e- -um in chor- -dis et or- -ga- -no lau- -da-
-te e- -um in chor- -dis et or- -ga- -no lau- -da-
312
-or- -ga- -no lau- -da- -te e- -um lau- -da-
-te e- -um lau- -da- -te
-te lau- -da- -te e- -um lau- -da-
318
e- -um lau- -da- -te in chor- -dis et or- -ga-
e- -um lau- -da- -te in chor- -dis et or- -ga-
-te e- -um lau- -da- -te lau- -da- -te lau-

324
-no lau - - - te e - um lau - da - -
-no lau - da - - te e - um lau -
-da - - - te e - um lau - da - - te in chor - dis
330
-te in chor - dis et
-da - - - - - - - te in chor - dis et
et or - ga - -no lau - da - - te e - um lau - da -
336
or - ga - -no lau - da - - - - -te
or - ga - -no lau - da - - - - -te lau
-te e - um lau - da - -te e - um lau - da -
342
lau - dc - - - -te lau - da - - - -
-da - - - -te e - um lau
-te in chor - dis et or - ga - -no lau - da - -te
348
-te e - um
-da - - - -te lau - da - - - -te lau
e - um lau - da -te lau - da - - - -te in

354
-te in chor- -dis et or- -ga- -no lau- -da-
-da- -te e- -um in chor- -dis et or- -ga- -no lau- -da-
chor- -dis et or- -ga- -no lau-
5
360
-te in chor- -dis et or- -ga-
-te in chor- -dis et or- -ga-
-da- -te e- -um lau- -da- -te lau- -da-
9 8 5 3 9 8 7 7 6 7 6
4 3 5 4 3 4
366
Da cappella
-no lau- -da- -te
-no lau- -da- -te
-te lau- -da- -te
7
3
371
Om- -nis spi- -ri- -tus lau-
376
Om- -nis spi- -ri- -tus lau- -det Do- -mi- -num om- -nis
-det lau- -det Do- -mi- -num lau- -det Do- -mi- -num
Om- -nis spi- -ri- -tus
4 #

spi- -ri- tus lau- det Do- -mi- -num lau- -
lau- -det Do- -mi- -num lau- -
lau- -det Do- -mi- -num lau- -det
-det Do- -mi- -num om- -nis
-det Do- -mi- -num lau- -det Do- -mi-
lau- -det Do- -mi- -num lau- -det Do- -mi-
spi- -ri- tus lau- -det lau- det Do- -mi- -num
-num lau- -det Do- -mi- -num
-num om- -nis spi- -ri- tus lau- -det Do- -mi- -num lau-
lau- -det lau- det Do- -mi- -num lau-
lau- -det lau- - -det lau- -det Do- -mi- -num
-det Do- -mi- -num
-det om- -nis spi- -ri- tus lau- -det Do- -mi-
om- -nis spi- -ri- tus lau- -det lau- -det Do- -mi-
om- -nis spi- -ri- tus lau- -det Do- -mi-